BRIDGE BASICS

By
Mary A. McVey

Edited by
Linda Roberts Bailey

A PUBLICATION OF KET

To the bridge partners
I have known and loved.

M. A. McV.

ISBN 0-910475-01-6

KET
600 Cooper Drive
Lexington
Kentucky 40502

TABLE OF CONTENTS

PREFACE

Welcome to the world of bridge!

If you haven't played before, you'll love it. And you can learn this fascinating game easily, taking one small step at a time. If you have played bridge, perhaps for years, a little brushup every now and then is good for all of us.

This game of contract bridge has a lot going for it! In the first place, it's fun. It's such a pleasant way to spend time with friends, and it's a great family game. You know, it really is easy. Anyone — man, woman, or child — who can count to 40 and pass second-grade arithmetic can learn to bid like an expert.

Another thing I love about bridge is that it's so cheap! Most forms of recreation cost a lot of money these days, but you can play bridge for weeks for the price of two decks of cards.

It's a universal game, too. No matter where you happen to be in this world, you'll find people eager to play. Once my husband and I had two hours to kill in the

Athens airport. There was another couple waiting for the same plane so we started a bridge game on a suitcase. Within five minutes we were surrounded by a dozen onlookers who obviously didn't speak the same language, but, just as obviously, loved bridge and wanted to watch.

Of course, the more you know about anything and the more proficient you become, the more fun it is. This is true of everything from golf to gardening, and most certainly is true of bridge.

In this little book we deal with the bare basics of bidding, but I hope it will whet your appetite for the game, and you'll go on to learn more and more about the fine points of bidding and play of the hand.

Remember, it's all for fun, so keep dealing the cards and ENJOY!

HOW TO USE THIS BOOK

The important points stressed in the "Bridge Basics" television series will be outlined and explained in this book. There is no need to spend time copying sample hands from the screen. All of the hands and their explanations used in the series will be included. There is space at the end of each chapter for your notes so that you can jot down information you particularly want to remember. We suggest that you take your notes here so that all of your information on bridge will be in one handy location.

After you have watched the lesson on television and read the corresponding chapter, you can check your understanding of the basics in the "Test Yourself" section at the end of each chapter. Try to find the answer to the problem and explain why you bid as you did, before looking at the explanations.

Now, let's take a look at some "Bridge Basics."

1
INTRODUCTION TO THE GAME

I'VE BEEN ASKED many times how in the world this game of bridge got started, so perhaps you'd like to know that contract bridge is the direct descendant — in fact the great-grandchild — of the ancient and scientific game of whist. In whist, the trump suit is determined by the dealer turning a card face up on the table. The child of whist was bridge, and the dealer had the privilege of naming the suit he wished to be trump, or, if he had no preference, he could "bridge it" across the table to his partner, who then named the trump suit. After bridge came auction bridge, and for the first time, all the players had a chance to bid for the right to decide which suit would be trump. As in any auction, the high bidder won. Auction bridge was followed by contract bridge, which is where we are today. In contract bridge, the bidding is all important, because the partnership may count toward game *only* the number of tricks it has contracted to take in the final bid. If you win the contract by bidding two of a suit and end up making

9

four, you may only score the two you bid toward the game.

You can see how vitally important bidding is, and that is what we shall concentrate on together. But before we start on the nitty-gritty, for the benefit of those who have never played, let's take a look at a deck of cards.

The Bridge Deck

There are 52 cards in a standard deck and the deck is divided into four suits: spades, hearts, diamonds, and clubs. Each suit contains 13 cards with ace the highest card and two the lowest. The ace, king, queen, jack, and ten of each suit are called the "honor cards" and we will be referring to these throughout the book. Each deck contains the following:

Spades ♠   ace, king, queen, jack, ten, nine, eight, seven, six, five, four, three, two

Hearts ♡   ace, king, queen, jack, ten, nine, eight, seven, six, five, four, three, two

Diamonds ◊   ace, king, queen, jack, ten, nine, eight, seven, six, five, four, three, two

Clubs ♣   ace, king, queen, jack, ten, nine, eight, seven, six, five, four, three, two

It is very important that you remember the rank of the suits. The spade suit is the highest ranking, followed in order by hearts, diamonds and then clubs, the lowest. Spades and hearts are called the "major suits" and diamonds and clubs are the "minor suits."

Ranking even higher than the spade suit is "no trump," which is played when the bidder has high cards in all suits and does not wish one suit to be more powerful than any other in playing the hand.

The suit rankings are extremely important during the bidding of the hands. If your opponent bids one of a suit and the suit you like ranks higher than his, you may outbid him by bidding just one of your suit. But if his suit is higher ranking than yours, you will have to bid two of your suit to beat his one bid. The reason we are so eager to win the bid is because if we have a suit with several cards, including some honor cards, we would very much like to be in charge of this particular deal and have our good suit be the "trump." If you have no cards in your hand of the suit the opponent plays, you may win a trick by playing a small trump card and capture the opponents' high cards.

Before we start on the bidding, let's see about the mechanics of the bridge game.

Bridge Play

It takes four people to play bridge, and before the game begins, a deck of cards is spread face down on the table and each player draws a card. The two who cut the high cards play together, and the two low cards play together. If two of you cut the same card, remember the suit rankings to determine which is the higher card.

The one thing I want you to remember always is that bridge is a *partnership game!* You and your partner are in this together through thick and thin and you will never — repeat never — dream of criticizing your partner in any way!

The player who cuts the high card "deals." He chooses his seat and his partner sits across the table. The person to the left of the dealer shuffles the deck, passes it to the player on the dealer's right, and he cuts the cards by taking approximately half the deck and

11

placing it toward the dealer. The dealer then places the remaining half of the deck on top, and begins the deal. You know, in bridge, everything goes to the left in a clockwise manner — the deal, the bidding, and the playing of the cards — so the dealer begins with the player on his left and distributes the cards, one at a time, to each player ending with himself. Each player will end up with 13 cards. During the deal, the partner of the dealer shuffles the other deck of cards and places it on his own right, ready for the player on his right to deal the next hand.

Each player picks up his cards and sorts them into suits, with the cards in each suit in numerical order. Most players separate the red suits from the black because it's less confusing. It's important to hold your cards close to your chest so nobody can see your hand.

The dealer has the first opportunity to bid. Whenever a player's hand is not good enough to bid, he merely says, "Pass." The player on his left then has the next chance to speak. Sometimes all four players pass, so the hand is discarded and there is another deal. But let's suppose that the dealer bids one of a suit. He is saying that he expects his hand and his partner's hand to take seven tricks if that particular suit is the trump suit. The first six tricks, called the "book," must be taken before you can count the tricks you have contracted to make. So, if your bid is four spades, you are contracting to take the book of six plus four more. The bidding proceeds around the table clockwise so that each player has the opportunity to speak. The bidding is over when there have been three consecutive passes, and the final bid wins the contract.

The partner who first bid the suit which won the contract is called the "declarer," and he plays the hand.

The opponent on declarer's left makes the first play, which is called the "opening lead," by placing a card face up on the table. This is a very important lead, and we'll talk about it in detail later. As soon as the lead is made, the partner of declarer places his cards face up on the table. putting the trump suit down first, followed by each of the other suits. Declarer plays his partner's hand as well as his own and the partner is called the "dummy."

Let's take a minute to talk about the dummy. He does not look into any of the other hands or speak at all except for one important function that he must perform. Each player must play from his hand a card of the same suit that was led. This is called "following suit." If ever the declarer does not follow suit, it is the duty of the dummy to say, "Partner, have you none?" and declarer will look at his hand again to be sure that he has no cards of the suit led. There is a big penalty for failing to follow suit if you can do so. Each player should check his partner the first time he fails to follow, but it is especially important for the dummy, as declarer is playing two hands and may be more apt to make a mistake.

Now, to get back to the opening lead. Each person plays in turn and when four cards have been played, that is called a "trick." Whoever wins the trick has the privilege of making the next lead, and so the game continues until all 13 tricks are taken. There are three ways tricks are won:

(1) With high cards.

(2) With trumps. When you can no longer follow suit, you may trump your opponents' trick with one of the suit that is the trump in that deal.

(3) With small cards. When all of the high cards in

that suit have already been played and nobody can trump, the smaller cards in that suit might take tricks.

Scoring

After a hand has been played, you write down the score. It is very wise for each player to keep score because it keeps you more alert about the status of the game.

It takes 100 points to make a "game," which is what we're always trying to do. We've discussed the major suits and minor suits, and you will see below the difference in scoring their value.

The scoring is as follows:

No trump } 40 points for the first trick over six
          30 points for each additional trick

Major suits
Spades } 30 points for each trick over six
Hearts

Minor suits
Diamonds } 20 points for each trick over six
Clubs

You can see that in order to get a game (100 points), you must bid and make three no trump, or four of a major suit, or five of a minor suit.

When one side has made a game, they are "vulnerable." This is a lovely state because it means you are half way toward making the "rubber," which is won by the partnership that scores two games. When one side wins the rubber, you then switch partners and start all over again.

There is a big bonus for winning the rubber (500 points if your side wins two out of three games and 700 points if your side wins two games before your opponents make a game). However, you should bid more carefully when you are vulnerable because the penalty for going "down" (failing to make your contract) is much stiffer than when you are "not vulnerable." All scoring that does not count toward game (bonuses, penalties, and tricks that you make *over* your bid) goes "above the line" on the score pad, and only the points that you bid and make go "below the line." Often your hand is not strong enough to bid a game, and the bidding stops at say three clubs. You make your three club bid, so you get 60 points below the line, which you will try to add to on the next hand and get your 100 points. This is called "part score."

Again, only the points that count toward game count below the line. All bonus and penalty points and tricks made but not bid are scored above the line. A typical bridge scorepad looks like this:

WE	THEY

A complete scoring table follows:

Scores above the line

Overtricks

	Not vulnerable	Vulnerable
Undoubled	Ordinary trick value	Ordinary trick value
Doubled	100 per trick	200 per trick
Redoubled	200 per trick	400 per trick

Additonal bonus

For making any doubled or redoubled contract   50

Honors

4 trump honors in any one hand	100
5 trump honors in any one hand	150
At no trump, 4 aces in one hand	150

Slam bonuses

	Not vulnerable	Vulnerable
Small slam	500	750
Grand slam	1000	1500

Penalties for undertricks

	Not vulnerable	Vulnerable
Undoubled	50 each trick	100 each trick
Doubled	100 for first trick, 200 for each additional trick	200 for first trick, 300 for each additional trick
Redoubled	Twice the doubled penalty	Twice the doubled penalty

Rubber bonus

When the rubber is won in two games	700
When the rubber is won by two games to one	500

Unfinished rubber

Bonus for a side with a game   300
Bonus for a part score in an unfinished game   50

Scores below the line

Spades or hearts   30 points for each trick over six
Diamonds or clubs   20 points for each trick over six
No trump   40 points for the first trick, 30 for
                                     each additional trick over six

If the contract has been doubled, multiply the trick score by 2; if redoubled, by 4.

Counting Your Hand

How can you tell exactly how good a hand is? It's really very easy because there is a definite value for each high card, and it's a matter of simple arithmetic! The tens don't have any point count, and of course the nines and eights don't, but they're lovely to have, and they sort of fatten up your hand and make you happier than if you held a bunch of twos, threes, and fours.

When you arrange your hand after the deal, count up your high cards by the points given below and get the total high card count of the hand.

High Card Points
Ace = 4 points
King = 3 points
Queen = 2 points
Jack = 1 point

Now, we come to something equally as important as the high cards and please never overlook it! It is the "distribution" of the hand. In other words, the shape of your hand makes a great big difference. So, if you have a suit with only two cards in it (we call this a "doubleton"), that is worth one point in value to your hand. If you have a suit with only one card (this is called a "singleton"), that is worth two additional points. And, if you are missing one suit entirely (called a "void"), add three points to your evaluation.

Distributional Points
Doubleton = 1 point
Singleton = 2 points
Void = 3 points

I always add up the points for high cards and then add the distributional points to get the total value of my hand. For goodness sake, if you must forget something, just forget to count one of your high cards, but don't forget to count your distribution. Unfortunately, some people do overlook it, and so never get the true value of their hand.

The examples below will show how very important this is.

Examples:

♠ K 7 2
♡ J 4 3
◇ A 8 7 6
♣ Q 8 5

Let's count this hand — three points for the king, one for the jack, four for the ace, and two for the queen, making a total of 10 points. Ten points is exactly average, as there are 40 high-card points in the deck. So, an average hand isn't valuable enough to get excited about.

18

♠ A 8 7 4 3 2   Now, let's count this hand. The
♡ (Void)   high-card points are exactly the
♢ K Q J 5 4 3   same — a total of 10 points —
♣ 4   but add three points for the void
and two points for the singleton
and you have a good 15-point
hand! This hand looks so much
better than the other one and,
of course, it is much better due
to distribution.

In the course of the bidding, if you and your partner
can figure that between you, the two hands have 26
points, they should be good enough for a game in no
trump or one of the major suits. It will take 29 points in
the combined hands to produce a game at a minor suit
because it takes your book of six plus five more tricks. If
the partnership has 33 points, it's worth trying for a
"small slam" (all of the tricks but one) and the bonus
you get when you bid and make a small slam is terrific
(500 points above the line if you are not vulnerable or
750 points above the line if you are vulnerable)! It's very
rare that you and your partner are able to bid a "grand
slam" (that's when you contract to take *all* the tricks) but
if you can do it, the bonus is 1,000 points if you are not
vulnerable and 1,500 points if you're vulnerable! Very
exciting!

And, you ask, how in the world do we figure how
many points are in *both* hands? Why, from the bidding,
which is the way that you and your partner talk to each
other and describe your hands!

In order to be a good bidder, the first thing you must
do is count your hand correctly, adding the high-card

count and the distributional count, so you will be accurate.

Just tuck these figures away in the back of your mind:

26 points = Game in a major suit or no trump
29 points = Game in a minor suit
33 points = Small slam
37 points = Grand slam

Of course, there's no double deluxe guarantee that these points will *always* produce what they're supposed to, as sometimes you have bad luck on a hand, but it's a sort of yardstick to go by.

We'll talk about bidding from now on, but there's one thing I want to caution you about, and I hope very much you'll never forget it. Please keep on your "poker face" at all times and *never*, by an expression, a tone of voice, a sigh, or a large grin, give anyone any idea of what your hand looks like. *We describe our hands by bidding only!* And remember, at the bridge table, your partner is the most important person in your life and partners are to love — not to criticize!

Test Yourself

Before looking at the answers, try to determine how many points each hand contains.

1. ♠ A Q 9 7
♡ Q 4 3
◊ Q 10 8 6
♣ K 4

Fourteen points — six points for the ace and queen of spades, two points for the queen of hearts, two points for the queen of diamonds, three points for the king of clubs and one point for the doubleton. Don't forget to count your distributional points!

2. ♠ Q 6 3   *Fifteen points.*
    ♡ A
    ◇ K Q J 8 4 3 2
    ♣ 10 8

3. ♠ A K Q 6   *Seventeen points.*
    ♡ 4 3
    ◇ Q 10 2
    ♣ K Q 10 8

4. ♠ J 10 8 4   *Two points.* Unfortunately,
    ♡ 8 6 3   hands like this are all too
    ◇ 4 2   common!
    ♣ 10 8 6 4

5. ♠ A K J 10   *Twenty-three points.*
    ♡ K Q 8
    ◇ A
    ♣ A 8 7 6 4

6. ♠ A K Q J 8 4 3 2 *Seventeen points.*
    ♡ (Void)
    ◇ K 3
    ♣ 10 8 6

7. ♠ J 10 8 4   *Seventeen points.*
    ♡ K Q 10
    ◇ A Q 6
    ♣ K Q 2

21

8. ♠ Q J 9 3 2   *Thirteen points.*
    ♡ K 4
    ◇ A 8 4 3 2
    ♣ 10

9. ♠ Q J 8 7 5 4 2   *Thirteen points.*
    ♡ A
    ◇ K 10
    ♣ 9 7 6

10. ♠ 8 7 3   *Fourteen points.*
    ♡ A K
    ◇ Q J 4 3 2
    ♣ K 4 2

11. ♠ (Void)   *Fourteen points.*
    ♡ K J 10 8 4 3 2
    ◇ Q 10 8 2
    ♣ A 4

12. ♠ Q 10 8 7 5 4 2 *Nine points.*
    ♡ 10
    ◇ Q 10 8 4 2
    ♣ (Void)

13. ♠ A Q 10 4   *Twelve points.*
    ♡ J 10 9 8
    ◇ K 8 4 3
    ♣ 2

14. ♠ A K Q   *Twenty-five points.*
    ♡ K J 10 8
    ◇ A 10
    ♣ A Q J 6

NOTES

NOTES

2

OPENING SUIT BIDS OF ONE
AND RESPONSES

THE BIG MAJORITY of hands at the bridge table are opened by someone bidding one of a suit, so we are going to concentrate now on that most frequently made bid.

By "opening bid" we mean the first bid that is made at the table. If your hand isn't strong enough to bid, you simply say, "Pass." Occasionally all four players will have to pass and then the hand is thrown away and the next dealer deals another hand.

Remember, you are *always* eager to open the bidding if at all possible so, as soon as the deal is over, pick up your cards and try like mad to open! If you have 13 points total in your hand (high-card and distributional points), *please* find something to bid! If you have as many as 14 points, it's an absolute MUST! It always makes your partner happy and your opponents sad when you open the bidding, so for goodness sake, don't miss an opportunity to do both.

The opening bid usually just starts the action, as other

people at the table will probably want to bid, too.

What Is A Biddable Suit?
1) Any five-card suit is biddable. And if you have more than five cards in a suit, it's even better! The more cards in a suit the merrier!

Examples:

♠ A 5
♡ 10 8 7 6 5
◇ A K 2
♣ Q 4 3

Open the bidding with one heart. You hold 14 points so you *must* open the bidding. Even though the heart suit doesn't have any high cards, ANY FIVE-CARD SUIT IS BIDDABLE!

♠ A K Q J 4
♡ 6 2
◇ Q 4 3
♣ Q 6 3

You have 15 points (don't forget to count your double-ton) so, of course, you open this hand one spade.

2) Any minor suit (diamonds or clubs) is biddable.

Examples:

♠ K Q 5
♡ A Q 3
◇ J 5 3 2
♣ Q 7 4

You have 14 points and must open the bidding. The diamond suit is weak, but it does have four cards and ANY MINOR SUIT IS BIDDABLE!

♠ A 6 3
♡ A Q 4
◇ K 10 6
♣ Q 6 4 2

With 15 points and a four-card minor suit, bid one club.

3) Only *good* four-card major suits (hearts or spades) are biddable. Major suits are very desirable because a game in a major suit is either four hearts or spades, while in a minor suit it takes five clubs or diamonds to make a game. Therefore, be very careful about opening a four-card major suit because you are telling you partner you have a *good* suit. I only open them if all of my strength is in the two major suits. Some people refuse to open four-card major suits. If your partner is one of these people, go along with him and only open a major if you have five cards in the suit. However, for our discussion, it is perfectly acceptable to open a good four-card major suit. You don't have to be so particular with the minor suits. Again, any minor suit is biddable — no matter how weak.

Example:

♠ K Q J 3	With 15 points and two good
♡ A K J 7	four-card major suits, open
◊ 8 7 5	the bidding with one spade
♣ 6 2	planning to bid hearts later.

4) Now we come to an opening bid that is most commonly called the short club but I prefer to call it the convenient club bid. Perhaps the convenient minor suit bid might be more descriptive because you can use it with either clubs or diamonds. It's nothing new. It's nothing fancy. And, it's nothing to get excited about, but, unfortunately, some people misunderstand and misuse it.

You sometimes have a hand that must open. The count is there, but the hand doesn't have a good opening bid. So, as a matter of convenience you choose to open with a bid of one in a three-card minor suit. If you don't have three clubs, you will have three diamonds. Remember, we have said that *any* minor suit may be opened, and when you open the bidding you aren't promising your partner a thing about the quality of that suit. You are merely saying, "Partner, I have a hand that is good enough to open the bidding."

Your partner is always eager to respond to any opening bid and, if he can, he certainly will. If he doesn't have the strength, of course he passes.

So, this bid is a very handy little gadget to use when you need it, but don't get uptight about it when your partner happens to open one club or one diamond. For heaven's sake, bid normally, and pass when necessary. After all, you don't know whether he has seven clubs or three.

Examples:

♠ Q 6 5 2
♡ Q 7 6 4
◊ A K
♣ Q 8 5

With 14 points, you must open the bidding, but both four-card major suits are weak and you don't have a four-card minor suit. Open the bidding with one club.

♠ Q 6 3 2
♡ J 10 8
◊ Q J 2
♣ A K J

Open the bidding with one club. The four-card major suit is too weak to bid.

Choice of Biddable Suits
1) What do you do if you're lucky enough to have two suits that are biddable? With two suits of unequal length, bid the longer suit first.

Examples:

♠ 7 2
♡ A K Q 4
◇ 7 2
♣ K J 8 3 2

You have 15 points and two biddable suits. Bid the five-card suit first, planning to bid the four-card heart suit later.

♠ A K 7 5 2
♡ 7
◇ K J 10 6 4 2
♣ 4

Again, with 15 points and two biddable suits, bid the six-card diamond suit before the five-card spade suit.

2) When you have two five-card suits, bid the higher ranking suit first.

Examples:

♠ Q 8 7 4 2
♡ A K 9 5 2
◇ 4
♣ K 3

Open the bidding with one spade even though the heart suit is the better suit. At the next opportunity you can bid hearts. If your partner has minimum count, he can either pass the heart bid or bid two spades, without raising the contract bid to the three level. If you open the bidding with one heart and then bid two spades, if your partner wants to support the hearts, he will have to bid at the three level.

♠ K J 6 5 3
♡ 4 2
◇ A Q J 4 2
♣ 7

Open the bidding with one spade. Always bid the higher ranking five-card suit first.

3) If you have two biddable four-card suits that don't touch in ranking order, bid the lower ranking suit first. This gives your partner the chance to bid another suit at the one level.

Examples:

♠ A K 6 3
♡ 9 5 3
◊ A 7
♣ Q 8 4 2

Bid one club. Even though the spade suit is better, open the bidding with one club, intending to bid the spade suit later. This gives your partner the opportunity to bid either diamonds or hearts at the one level.

♠ K Q J 2
♡ 6 4
◊ A Q 4 3
♣ Q 8 6

Open the bidding with the lower ranking diamond suit and bid the spade suit at the next opportunity.

4) If you have two biddable four-card suits that touch each other in ranking order, bid the higher ranking suit first.

Example:

♠ 7 6 5
♡ 8 2
◊ K J 5 2
♣ A K Q 4

Open the bidding with one diamond. Let's say your partner responds with one heart. You can then bid two clubs and give your partner an easy choice of your suits. He can either pass two clubs or if he prefers diamonds, he may bid two diamonds without getting the bidding too high. If you

31

do it the wrong way and open the bidding with one club rather than the correct one diamond bid and your partner responds one heart, you would then bid two diamonds. If your partner then prefers clubs, he would have to bid clubs at the three level.

Don't worry if .all this seems a little complicated. Of course it will at first, but you'll get used to it. If you just remember that you and your partner want to bid as much as possible without letting the bidding get too high, it will make sense to you.

Responses To Opening Bids

When your partner opens the bidding, you are delighted that his hand is that good and you can hardly wait to respond to him and bid something, if at all possible.

0-5 points

If you can't find at least six points in high cards and distributional points, pass!

Examples:

♠ 8 6 5 3
♡ 4 3
◊ 10 9 8 4 3
♣ 6 5

Your partner opens the bidding with one club. Unfortunately, hands like this do happen to all of us and you should pass them without hesitation.

♠ Q 8 6 3
♡ J 10 8
◊ J 6 5 2
♣ 4 3

Your partner opens the bidding with one heart and you only have five points. You should pass.

6-9 points (minimum range)

If you have at least six points, you *must* respond to your partner's opening bid. In the six-to-nine-point minimum range, you have three options:

1) You can bid another suit if you can bid it at the one level. This is what you'd prefer to do.

2) You can raise your partner's suit. We hate to raise partner's minor suit, but love to raise his major.

3) You can bid one no trump. When you can do neither of the other choices, bid one no trump.

When you raise your partner's suit or bid one no trump, you are telling your partner that you have only the minimum count to respond to his bid. If you bid another suit you could have as few as six points or a very good hand. *If you have six to nine points, you should choose to bid only once.*

Examples:

♠ Q 5 3 2
♡ 9 6 4 3
◊ Q 6 4 2
♣ 9

Your partner opens the bidding with one club and with six points, you must respond. Bid one diamond.

In the following cases your partner has opened the bidding with one diamond.

♠ K Q 6 3 2
♡ 10 6 4
◊ Q 6 2
♣ 4 3

You have eight points and a good five-card major suit. Bid one spade.

♠ K 6 3
♡ Q 4 2
♢ J 10 7
♣ Q 10 8 6

You have eight points and even distribution. Bid one no trump.

♠ 6 4 3
♡ 10 5
♢ K J 4 3
♣ Q 10 8 2

You can support your partner's diamond suit and you only have seven points. Bid two diamonds.

10-12 points

With 10-12 points, you are good enough to bid another suit, even if your suit ranks lower than your partner's and you have to bid at the two level. And you may also bid twice. In the following examples your partner has opened the bidding with one spade:

Examples:

♠ Q 7 4
♡ 6 3
♢ K Q J 7 4
♣ Q 5 2

You are in the 10-12 point range with the good five-card diamond suit. Bid two diamonds.

♠ 10 5 4
♡ A K Q 6 2
♢ Q 4 3
♣ 10 2

Bid two hearts over partner's one spade bid.

13-15 points

When you have 13-15 points and you know your partner has at least 13 points to open the bidding, together you have at least 26 points and probably a game somewhere. You have several options:

1) You can bid a new suit at the one or two level.

2) You can jump raise your partner's suit (in other words if your partner bids one heart, and you have support in hearts, your bid is three hearts). When you are going to raise your partner's suit you may promote an honor one point (you may not promote an ace) because, for instance, a jack in the suit your partner bid is certainly more valuable than a jack in another suit! If you have four of his trumps you may promote your distributional values too. (A singleton counts three instead of two and a void suit five instead of three. Your doubletons may not be promoted.)

Example:

♠ **Q 7 4 2**   Partner opens with a spade.
♡ **A 6 3**   You know you are going to
◇ **7**   support the spade suit. Un-
♣ **K 7 6 5 2**   til you revalue your hand you
                       only have 11 points. When
                       you add one point for the
                       queen and one point for the
                       singleton, you have 13 points
                       and can jump partner's suit to
                       three spades

3) You can bid *two* no trump if you have even distribution and 13-15 high card points.
    In the following cases your partner has opened the bidding with one heart:

♠ K Q 6
♡ Q 5 3 2
◇ 10
♣ A 10 4 3 2

Bid three hearts. In this case, there is no reason to bid two clubs. Your partner has bid at least a good four-card suit and you have good support in the hearts. You revalue your hand and promote the queen to three points instead of two and the singleton to three points instead of two and your hand is now worth 15 points.

♠ K Q 4
♡ Q 9 2
◇ Q 7 5 2
♣ A 6 3

Bid two no trump. You have opening high card count with even distribution. You have described your hand perfectly.

♠ K Q 8
♡ 10 4
◇ A K Q 7 6
♣ 8 6 4

Show your good five-card suit. Bid two diamonds.

16-18 points

If you hold 16-18 points, there should be at least a game somewhere with the strong possibility of a slam.

Examples:

♠ K J 5 2
♡ A 6
◇ 6 4
♣ A K 9 5 4

Partner opens with one spade. With 17 points, you would change suits and bid two clubs. Let's say your partner rebids his spade suit at two spades. You would then jump to four spades. This hand is too good to immediately jump to three spades.

♠ A K 4
♡ K Q 10
◊ 10 8 6
♣ K J 10 8

Partner opens with one diamond. With 16 points, you immediately jump to three no trump.

Over 18 points
This is gorgeous!
You are looking for a slam. You can show your partner you have over 18 points by a jump shift. A jump shift means that you change suits and bid one more than is necessary. For instance, your partner bids a club and you bid two spades. You have changed the suit and bid one more than you need to bid since the logical bid over one club is *one* spade.

Examples:

♠ A Q 2
♡ A K Q 4 3 2
◊ K 6 5
♣ 4

Your partner opens the bidding with one diamond. You have 20 points. To show your good suit and point count, bid *two* hearts.

♠ Q 10 8
♡ A K Q
◊ 10
♣ A Q J 4 3 2

Your partner opens the bidding with one diamond. Your jump shift bid is *three* clubs.

37

Test Yourself

In the following cases, you are the dealer. Before looking at the answers, try to determine your opening bid.

1. ♠ Q 6 3
   ♡ A K 6
   ◇ J 10 8 3
   ♣ Q 6 3

   Pass. With only 12 points, you don't have the necessary 13 points to open the bidding.

2. ♠ A K
   ♡ Q 6 4 2
   ◇ Q 10 8 3
   ♣ Q 6 2

   One diamond. Your four-card heart suit is not strong enough to open, but any minor suit is biddable.

3. ♠ 10 9 8 6 3
   ♡ K Q 10
   ◇ A K
   ♣ Q 6 5

   One spade. Even though it is not a strong spade suit there are five cards in the suit and any five-card suit is biddable.

4. ♠ J 10 8 2
   ♡ Q 6 3
   ◇ Q 6 3
   ♣ A K Q

   One club. When you don't have a biddable four-card suit, open with the convenient minor suit bid.

5. ♠ A Q J 10 6
   ♡ 10
   ◇ 8
   ♣ A J 6 4 3 2

   One club. When you have two biddable suits, always bid the longer suit first.

38

6. ♠ K Q J 3
   ♡ A Q 6 3
   ◇ 10 6
   ♣ Q 6 3

   One spade. If you have two four-card suits that touch each other in ranking order, bid the higher ranking suit first.

7. ♠ K Q J 6
   ♡ 6 2
   ◇ A 10 3
   ♣ Q J 10 8

   One club. If you have two four-card suits that don't touch each other in ranking order, bid the lower ranking suit first.

8. ♠ A J 6 3 2
   ♡ 4
   ◇ A K 10 6 5
   ♣ 10 6

   One spade. If you have two five-card suits, bid the higher ranking suit first.

9. ♠ A K J 6 3
   ♡ 4
   ◇ 10 9
   ♣ J 10 9 8 3

   Pass. Your point count is not sufficient to open the bidding.

10. ♠ 10 4
    ♡ A Q J 5 2
    ◇ Q 3 2
    ♣ K 3 2

    One heart. Any five-card suit is biddable.

11. ♠ 10 8
    ♡ K J 8 4
    ◇ A K J 10 8
    ♣ 7 4

    One diamond. If you have two biddable suits, bid the longer suit first.

In the following cases, your partner has opened the bidding with one diamond and your opponent has passed. What is your bid?

12. ♠ 7 6 3 2
♡ Q J 4
◇ K J 10 6
♣ 10 2

Two diamonds. Raising your partner's suit to the two level shows minimum count and support for his suit.

13. ♠ J 8 4 2
♡ Q 10 6 3
◇ 10 8
♣ J 10 8

Pass. You must have six points to respond to your partner's opening bid.

14. ♠ K Q 10 6 3
♡ 10 2
◇ A 4 3
♣ J 4 2

One spade. Then plan to bid again showing that you have more than a minimum response.

15. ♠ K Q 2
♡ Q 7 4
◇ 10 9 8
♣ J 10 9 2

One no trump. This is a minimum response showing six to nine points and even distribution.

16. ♠ 9 4 3
♡ K 6
◇ 10 9 8
♣ A K J 10 6

Two clubs. You have a good five-card suit and sufficient strength to bid at the two level.

17. ♠ K 3
♡ Q 10 8
◇ A K 6 4 3
♣ J 10 8

Three diamonds. You can jump in your partner's suit with opening count.

18. ♠ Q 10 6
    ♡ A K 4
    ◊ K 10 8
    ♣ Q 6 3 2

    Two no trump. With balanced distribution and 13-15 high card points, two no trump describes your hand to your partner.

19. ♠ K 6
    ♡ A Q 2
    ◊ 10
    ♣ A K J 10 6 3 2

    Three clubs. You jump and shift suits to tell your partner you have over 18 points. This is an invitation to your partner to look for slam.

NOTES

41

NOTES

3

NO TRUMP BIDS AND RESPONSES

N₀ TRUMP BIDDING is a horse of a different color! It is so
exact that your second-grade arithmetic makes it almost
foolproof, and you and your partner can describe both
the strength and the shape of your hands.

No trump means just what it says. During the play of
the hand, there is no trump suit. The highest card
played in the suit on each trick wins the trick.

Requirements For No Trump Opening

There are two requirements to open the bidding at no
trump and they are equally important — (1) balanced
distribution and (2) high-card points.

Balanced distribution

There are only three acceptable no trump distribution
patterns. The X's below show numbers of cards in each
suit. It makes no difference which suit has four cards or
five cards — it's the overall shape of the hand that mat-
ters. *DON'T EVEN CONSIDER OPENING IN NO*

*TRUMP UNLESS YOU HAVE ONE OF THESE PAT-
TERNS:*

4-3-3-3	4-4-3-2	5-3-3-2
XXXX	XXXX	XXXXX
XXX	XXXX	XXX
XXX	XXX	XXX
XXX	XX	XX

High-card points
   When you count your hand for no trump, *YOU COUNT HIGH CARDS ONLY.* Never count distributional points in no trump because doubletons and singletons are a liability instead of an asset when no suit is trump.

Opening No Trump Bidding

   Bid one no trump with the correct balanced distribution, 16-18 high-card points and high cards in *three* of the four suits. If your hand contains a doubleton, it is comforting for it to be headed by at least the queen.

Examples:

♠ Q J 5 2
♡ K 8
◊ Q 3 2
♣ A K J 4

This is a perfect one no trump opening hand — 16 points, 4-4-3-2 distribution and high cards in all suits. You have described your hand perfectly to your partner!

♠ A K 10
♡ A Q 6
◊ J 8 6 3 2
♣ A 4

This is a maximum 18-point opening one no trump hand. Note that when counting the points, the distributional point for the doubleton is not counted.

Bid *two no trump* with the correct balanced distribution, 22-24 high-card points and high cards in all of the suits

Examples:

♠ K 9 5 ♡ A K Q ◊ A K J ♣ K 8 5 4	You have 23 high-card points, even 4-3-3-3 distribution and high cards in all suits. Open the bidding with two no trump.
♠ A K J 4 ♡ K Q 5 2 ◊ A Q 4 ♣ A J	This hand has 24 high-card points — another perfect two no trump opener.

Bid *three no trump* with the correct balanced distribution, 25-26 high-card points and high cards in all of the suits. Remember, it takes 26 high card points to make game in a no trump (three no trump). You are telling your partner you think you can make a game in your hand with little or no help.

Examples:

♠ A K Q ♡ A K J 6 ◊ K Q J 3 ♣ K 7	Twenty-six high-card points, even distribution and high cards in all suits — open this hand with three no trump.

♠ A Q 3　　　　　Even though you have a five-
♡ K Q 10　　　　card suit, open the bidding
♢ A Q　　　　　with three no trump.
♣ A K Q 4 3

I'm sure you're wondering about those lovely hands that contain 19-21 high-card points and no trump distribution. *DON'T BID NO TRUMP.* You are too strong to bid one no trump and not strong enough to bid two no trump. Bid one of a suit. No matter what your partner responds, jump to two no trump with 19 points and to three no trump with 20-21 points. Remember, your partner must have at least six points to respond to your bid and, if you have 20 points, together you have at least 26 points or game in no trump.

Examples:

♠ A 4　　　　　With 19 high-card points,
♡ K J 3　　　　open the bidding with one
♢ Q J 6　　　　club. If your partner makes a
♣ A K J 4 2　　response, you can then jump
　　　　　　　　to two no trump.

♠ K Q J　　　　With 21 high-card points,
♡ A J 6　　　　open the bidding with one
♢ K Q J 10　　diamond. If partner makes
♣ A 10 2　　　any response, you can jump
　　　　　　　　to game in three no trump.
　　　　　　　　Remember, he must have six
　　　　　　　　points to respond and you
　　　　　　　　have 21 points. Added to-
　　　　　　　　gether this 27 point count
　　　　　　　　should produce game.

47

Responses To Opening One No Trump Bid

Responding in a suit

In the following cases, your partner has bid one no trump and you do not have no trump distribution. The three examples listed below are *extremely important!*

Examples:

♠ 9 7 5
♡ J 9 7 5 4 3
♢ Q 7 3
♣ 7

Bid two hearts. This is a miserable hand. It's so bad that your partner won't have a ghost of a chance to make one no trump. So it's up to you to tell him so! Whenever the partner of the no trump opener bids two spades, two hearts, or two diamonds, he is saying, "Partner, my hand is terrible, but with your high cards, we will have a better chance playing the hand in my long suit. For heaven's sake, don't bid again!"

♠ K 6
♡ A Q 7 6 2
♢ 4 3
♣ 9 4 3 2

Bid three hearts. You have plenty of count to raise partner's no trump, but the wrong distribution. With two doubletons and a five-card suit, your hand will probably play better in a suit, so describe your hand to your partner and let him decide whether to play three no trump or four hearts.

♠ A 6 2
♡ J 10 8 7 4 3
♢ K 5 2
♣ 7

Bid four hearts. You *know* the hand will play better in a suit and your partner's 16-18 points added to your 10 points gives you at least 26 points and a shot at game. Don't worry about your weak suit. Remember, your partner bid no trump so he has something in the suit, and you're in good shape.

Stayman club convention

The Stayman club convention is a wonderful gadget which has nothing to do with clubs. When your partner opens the bidding with one no trump and you bid two clubs, you are simply asking, "Partner, do you have a four-card major suit with a high card in it?" You only use the Stayman bid when you have sufficient point count to raise your partner's no trump, but you are trying to find out whether the hand will play better at three no trump or at four hearts or spades because your hand can support *either* major suit. If your partner has four cards in a major suit, he bids it and you can go to game in that suit. If your partner bids two diamonds, he tells you he doesn't have a four-card major suit. You can then raise his no trump. You never bid hearts or spades yourself unless you have a *five-card suit.* Your partner then decides where the game should be played.

Example:

♠ K 7 5 2
♡ Q J 6 3
♢ A 6
♣ 7 3 2

Partner opens with one no trump. You can bid three no trump with 10 high-card points, but the hand might

49

play better in a major suit.
Bid two clubs to find out
whether your partner has a
four-card major suit.

NOTE: If you have one of those dreadful hands with no count and a singleton which would be sheer misery for your partner's no trump, and your six-card suit happens to be clubs, you'll just have to bid two clubs, and when your partner responds, you then bid three clubs. He will get the dreary picture and, of course, pass. You'll still be better off than you would have been at one no trump.

Responding in no trump

To raise your partner's opening no trump bid, *YOU SHOULD HAVE 4-3-3-3, 4-4-3-2 OR 5-3-3-2 NO TRUMP DISTRIBUTION YOURSELF.*

0-6 high-card points — Pass. Your partner has opened the bidding with one no trump. You have no trump distribution. Here's where your arithmetic comes in. You can count on him for 16 to 18 points, but even if he should have 18, if your hand has only six high-card points or less, there is no future to the hand. Of course, you would pass.

7 high-card points and a good five-card suit — You may raise to two no trump.

8-9 high-card points — Raise to two no trump. If partner has the maximum 18-point no trump opener, he will bid three no trump. If he has a minimum 16 points, he will pass.

10-14 high-card points — Raise to three no trump. Partner's 16 points added to your 10 points equal 26 points and game.

15-16 high-card points — Raise to four no trump. Your partner will know how many points you have and he will add them to his points and decide whether or not to bid six.

17-18 high-card points — Raise to six no trump (small slam). Just add your points to your partner's and you know you have it.

When your partner opens the bidding with two no trump, and you have four high-card points and even distribution, bid three no trump because he has 22 points and only needs your four points for the game. If you can add your points to your partner's and come up with 33 points, jump to six no trump.

Examples:

♠ Q 5 4
♡ 9 7 5 4
◊ 7 3 2
♣ Q 8 5

Partner has at least 22 points and you have four points for at least 26 points and game in no trump. Bid three no trump.

♠ Q J 10 4
♡ A 8 4
◊ Q 7 3
♣ Q 4 3

Your 11 points added to partner's 22 points should produce a small slam. Jump to six no trump.

Test Yourself

You are the dealer. Before looking at the answers, try to determine what your opening bid will be.

1. ♠ A 6 4 2
   ♡ J 3 2
   ◊ K Q 6
   ♣ J 10 8

Pass. You are too weak to open the bidding in a suit or in no trump.

2. ♠ K Q 6
♡ A Q 3
◇ A J 4 2
♣ 10 8 7

One no trump. You hold 16 high-card points, 4-3-3-3 distribution, and high cards in three of the four suits.

3. ♠ 10 9 8
♡ 8 7 6
◇ A Q J
♣ A K Q J

One club. The points and distribution suggest no trump but you must have high cards in three suits to bid no trump.

4. ♠ A J 9 8
♡ A J 6
◇ A K 10 6
♣ K 6

One diamond. With 20 high-card points you are too strong to bid one no trump and not strong enough to bid two no trump. You can jump to no trump later.

5. ♠ A J 10 9
♡ A K 6
◇ K Q 4 2
♣ A K

Two no trump. The perfect no trump bid with 24 points, 4-4-3-2 distribution and high cards in all suits.

6. ♠ A K Q
♡ K Q 10 4
◇ A K 8
♣ K Q 10

Three no trump. You hold 26 points. With no help from your partner you should have a good shot at making a three no trump game.

Your partner has opened the bidding with one no trump and your opponent has passed. What is your bid?

7. ♠ A 6 2
♡ J 8 7 6
♢ 10 9 8
♣ 7 5 2

Pass. The hand will not play better in a suit and your partner's 16-18 points added to your five points will not produce game.

8. ♠ A J 10 8
♡ Q 6 5 2
♢ 10 6 3
♣ K 2

Two clubs. This is the perfect hand for the Stayman club convention.

9. ♠ 8
♡ J 8 5 3
♢ Q J 10 8 6 2
♣ 10 8

Two diamonds. You are telling your partner you have a bad hand but it will definitely play better in this suit. Your partner *must* pass your bid.

10. ♠ K J 8 7 6 2
♡ K 2
♢ Q J 8 3
♣ 10

Four spades. Don't make your partner guess what you have. You know by adding your points to your partner's that you have enough points for game and you *know* that the hand will play better in a suit.

11. ♠ A 8 6 2
    ♡ K 10 3
    ◊ Q 6 2
    ♣ Q 10 8

Three no trump. Add your 11 points to your partner's 16-18 points and you should have a game at three no trump.

12. ♠ K Q 6
    ♡ A Q J 4
    ◊ K J 3
    ♣ Q 10 2

Six no trump. Your 18 points added to your partner's 16-18 points should produce a small slam.

13. ♠ J 4
    ♡ 10 2
    ◊ 7 6 5
    ♣ Q J 10 8 6 3

Two clubs. Your partner will think this is a Stayman club convention and will bid accordingly. You then bid three clubs to tell your partner you have a weak hand and a long club suit.

Your partner has opened the bidding with two no trump and your opponent has passed. What is your bid?

14. ♠ 10 8 5
    ♡ Q J 7 4
    ◊ Q 8 4
    ♣ 8 7 6

Three no trump. Your five points added to your partner's 22-24 points add up to at least 26 points or game at three no trump.

54

15. ♠ K J 6 3
   ♡ Q 6 2
   ◇ K 4 2
   ♣ Q 8 2

Six no trump. Your 11 points added to your partner's 22-24 points add up to at least 33 points or a small slam at no trump.

NOTES

NOTES

NOTES

4
OVERCALLS

Until now we've been talking about the opening bidder and his partner but let's face it, those two other people at the table haven't lost the power of speech and they will be in there competing. So let's see what happens when the opponents open the bidding. The term "overcall" means just what it says — a call over the opponent's bid.

Here are your six possibilities:

1. Pass — too many people don't avail themselves of the opportunity to pass when they should.

2. Simple overcall — this is the bid of another suit made as cheaply as possible.

3. Jump overcall — this is a bid that is higher than necessary over your opponent's opening bid.

4. Take-out double — a very valuable call which says you have enough strength to have opened the bidding yourself.

5. No trump — exactly the same hand you would have opened one no trump.

6. Cue Bid — very rare! The *strongest* of overcalls.

Pass

When you overcall the opponent's opening bid, you are promising nothing about the count of your hand, but *you are promising a good suit.* So, if your hand contains less than 13 points and you don't have a good five-card suit, *YOU PASS!* We *NEVER* overcall with a four-card suit no matter how strong it is.

Examples:

♠ K Q 3
♡ K 9 6 2
◊ 5 3 2
♣ A 7 4

The opponents have opened the bidding with a club. You should pass. Even though you have 12 points, your heart suit is very weak and only has four cards. When you over-call, you are not promising strong point count, only a good suit.

♠ 7 6 2
♡ A K Q 8
◊ 7 4
♣ K 9 4 3

Your opponents have opened with a diamond. You should pass. The hearts are lovely but there are only four of them. Don't stretch the five-card rule and bid the heart suit, even though it is tempting!

♠ Q 10 5 3
♡ A 9 8 7 2
◊ A 4
♣ Q 2

Your opponents have opened with one spade and you have a very nice opening hand, but you should pass because your heart suit is not strong and if you bid two hearts and the opponents have all the high hearts, you could be in serious trouble. Your hand is good enough so that you know your opponents probably can't make a game in spades.

Simple Overcall

A simple overcall means you are bidding your suit at the lowest possible level over your opponent's bid. An overcall makes no promises about the count of the hand. Again, don't overcall unless you have at least a *good five-card suit.* If you can stay at the one level with a simple overcall, your hand need not be as strong as if you are forced to go to the two level because when you bid one, you only have to take the book of six tricks plus one. Just remember, at the two level you are promising to take a book of tricks plus two (or eight tricks) so you need more than if you are only bidding at the one level.

Examples:

♠ 5 3
♡ 7 4 3
◇ K Q J 7 5 2
♣ 8 5

The opponents open the bidding with one club. Because you have a good six-card suit and you can stay at the one level, you can overcall with one diamond. You do not have enough strength to overcall at the two level if the opponents had bid one heart or one spade.

60

♠ 10 4
♡ K Q J 9 5
♢ 10 8 3
♣ A 6 2

The opponents open the bidding with one spade. You have a good strong heart suit. Your overcall bid is two hearts.

Jump Overcall

When you make a jump overcall, you bid your suit at a much higher level than necessary over the opponent's opening bid. Your hand is *very weak* and you could never have opened the bidding at the one level yourself. But, you have a lovely long suit and by bidding your suit high, you can really mess up the opponents and make it hard for them to bid their hands. Please don't let this business of bidding high on a weak hand bother you. *You don't expect to make the bid* — but you are happy to be set in a good cause. You are making a sacrifice because you feel that your opponents probably have the point count to make a game at some contract. You are trying to make it more difficult for them to find a suit because their next bids would be at such high levels. *Bid as high as you possibly can because you will bid only one time.* Plan to be set three tricks if you are not vulnerable, and two tricks if your side has already scored a game.

With any help at all from your partner, you actually stand a chance of making your jump overcall bid, but that's not your reason for doing so.

Examples:

♠ K Q J 10 7 5 2
♡ 2
♢ 5 3 2
♣ 7 4

Your opponents have opened the bidding with one heart and you are not vulnerable. Your jump overcall bid is

61

three spades which will make the partner of the opener have to bid four if he bids, and you hope he will not be able to. If you get the bid and the opponents don't double, play it happily and be prepared to go down in the contract. If the opponents bid over the three spade bid, *don't bid again*, no matter how tempting it might be to rebid your suit.

♠ 6
♡ 6 3
◊ A K Q 10 4 3 2
♣ 9 4 3

Your opponents open the bidding with one heart and you are not vulnerable. The jump overcall bid for this hand would be *four* diamonds. The hand will take at least seven tricks (all of the diamonds will probably be good) so the most you would be set is three tricks. In this case, the sacrifice would be well worth it.

♠ 2
♡ K Q J 10 6 4
◊ Q 10 8
♣ 8 6 5

Your opponents have opened the bidding with one diamond and you are not vulnerable. Your jump overcall bid is *two* hearts.

Take-out Double
There are two different kinds of doubles in bridge —

the penalty double and the take-out double — and they mean entirely different things. The penalty double is made when you think the opponents have bid more than they can make. You double and if they don't make the contract, you receive bonus points. But we will forget that at the moment because here we are interested in the take-out double which is one of our possibilities when the opponents open, and it has absolutely nothing to do with trying to defeat the opponents' contract. It simply forces your partner to bid.

But, you say, how in the world can you tell the difference in the two when you say double for either one. It is very simple, really, if you will remember this: *any double which is made at the doubler's first opportunity and before his partner has bid is a take-out double.* You must think very carefully when your partner doubles and ask yourself two questions — "Is this my partner's first chance to double?" and "Have I bid anything yet?" You might have passed previously, but it's a take-out double unless you have bid. Your partner might have bid, but if it is his first opportunity to double and you have not bid, it is definitely a take-out double.

The take-out double says, "Partner, I have a good hand and would have opened the bidding myself if the opponents hadn't beat me to it, so bid your longest suit, please." Your partner *must* bid his long suit even without a face card in his hand. The only time the partner of the doubler may pass with a weak hand is when there has been an intervening bid by the partner of the opener. If the partner of the doubler is *sure* that his hand combined with his partner's is strong enough to set the contract, he may also pass.

Examples:

♠ 4 3
♡ K Q 3 2
◇ A 6 5
♣ A J 7 4

Your opponents have opened the bidding with one spade, and you have 15 points. You can't overcall with a suit because you have only four-card suits. Your correct bid is to double at your first opportunity and force your partner to bid his longest suit. You can support any suit he bids.

♠ 8 3
♡ K Q J 7 5 3
◇ A Q 5
♣ K 2

Your opponents have opened the bidding with one club. At first glance, it would appear that you should overcall with one heart but that wouldn't tell your partner that you have such a strong hand. You should double one club and your partner will know you have an opening bid. You can then bid your heart suit later and that will describe your hand perfectly.

No Trump

A no trump bid over the opponent's opening bid requires balanced no trump distribution, 16-18 high-card points and high cards in three of the four suits. In addition, you must have high cards in the opponent's suit. In other words, you must be able to stop the opponents from taking too many tricks in the suit they bid.

Examples:

♠ K J 8
♡ A Q 7 6
◇ J 5 3
♣ A Q 7

The opponents open the bidding with one heart. With 17 high-card points, even distribution and high cards in hearts, your correct bid is one no trump.

♠ A J 6
♡ Q 9 3
◇ K 4 3
♣ A K 7 4

The opponents open the bidding with one spade. Your bid of one no trump describes your hand perfectly to your partner.

Cue Bid

The cue bid is the immediate overcall in the same suit the opponents have opened. For example, your opponents bid one spade and you then bid two spades. This is the strongest bid you can make, and you are telling you partner you have a gorgeous hand and he is *forced* to keep bidding until your partnership reaches game. Your partner must then bid his longest suit. Again, once the cue bid is made, neither partner may pass the bidding until game is reached (unless you decide it would be more profitable to double the opponents and set their bid). The take-out double forces partner to bid once but the cue bid forces him to keep bidding until game is reached, so the cue bidder must practically have a game in his own hand as his partner may have no points at all.

Example:

♠ K Q J 5
♡ A Q J 5
◇ (Void)
♣ A K J 9 5

The opponents open the bidding with one diamond. Your bid is two diamonds to force your partner to bid his longest suit. With the cue bid, you tell your partner — "We've got game! Just give me the suit!"

Test Yourself

In the following cases, your opponents have opened the bidding with one diamond and you are not vulnerable. Before looking at the answers, try to determine your overcall bid.

1. ♠ 6
   ♡ A Q 10 8 6 3 2
   ◇ 6 4 3
   ♣ 8 7

Three hearts. Don't give your opponents the opportunity to find their suit at a low level. Jump overcall with three hearts and be prepared to go down in the contract. If your partner has anything at all, you actually have a chance at making the bid.

2. ♠ 10 9 8
   ♡ K Q 6 2
   ◇ J 7 6 3
   ♣ A 2

Pass. You have 11 points but no five-card suit. Remember, never overcall with a four-card suit.

66

3. ♠ J 6 2
   ♡ A K 10 6 3
   ◊ 6 5 4
   ♣ 10 8

One heart. You only have nine points but you can overcall at the one level.

4. ♠ A Q 10 8 3
   ♡ K J 4
   ◊ 10 8
   ♣ A 10 8

Double. You could bid one spade over the one diamond bid but your partner would think you had a good suit and few points. When you double the bid, you are telling your partner you have opening count. When your partner responds, you can bid your spade suit. The take-out double is a far more descriptive bid.

5. ♠ A 3 2
   ♡ A Q 10
   ◊ A J 3 2
   ♣ K 6 4

One no trump. You have the correct balanced distribution, 18 high-card points and two high cards in the opponent's diamond suit.

6. ♠ A K Q 4
   ♡ K Q 6 3
   ◊ 2
   ♣ A K J 4

Two diamonds. The cue bid forces your partner to bid his longest suit and is forcing to both partners until they reach game.

7. ♠ A Q 6 3
   ♡ A K 2
   ◊ 10 8 2
   ♣ K 6 3

Double. Don't bid one no trump even though you have balanced distribution and 16 points. You don't have high cards in the opponent's suit.

8. ♠ K Q 10 8 6 5 4 3
   ♡ 3 2
   ◊ 8
   ♣ 10 6

Three spades. Your eight-card suit is worthless unless you play the hand and if you give the opponents the opportunity to find a suit, they will probably play a contract at game. Don't give them the chance if you can help it!

9. ♠ A 10 9 8
   ♡ K Q J 2
   ◊ 8 4
   ♣ K 6 4

Double. Force your partner to name the suit. You can support any suit he bids.

10. ♠ 4 3 2
   ♡ 6
   ◊ 10 9
   ♣ A K Q 10 8 4 3

Four clubs. This is another example of the jump over-call.

11. ♠ K 2
   ♡ J 4 2
   ◊ 10 6 5
   ♣ A K 10 6 3

Two clubs. You have a good five-card club suit and enough strength to overcall at the two level.

NOTES

NOTES

71

5
REBIDS

THE REBID is when you get a second crack at the bidding. It has gone around the table and is back to you again.

Believe me, rebids will separate the sheep from the goats! This is probably the one thing in bridge that gives the average player the most trouble. And I can certainly understand why, as the bidding is sometimes pretty difficult.

But, you can save a lot of grief if you THINK AHEAD.

If you open the bidding, start thinking then about what you will probably do next time in various situations. You can figure right then whether your hand is minimum, good, or sensational.

When you open the bidding all you say to your partner is that you have enough points to open — period. Now, the second go-round is when you start describing your hand to your partner.

Remember, you can see your cards, but your partner

can't, so it's your job to make your hand *sound* to your partner the way it *looks* to you! Please don't make it sound weak if it's good. And please don't make it sound strong if it's minimum.

Remember, too, that any time you have opened the bidding and your partner changes the suit, you *must* bid again.

Before we start talking about rebids of the hand, I'd like to discuss rebidding a suit. When we say rebid a suit we mean bidding it twice *without* any assistance from partner. Remember, *any* six-card suit is rebiddable, a *strong* five-card suit is rebiddable and *no* four-card suit is rebiddable.

Please do not be confused on this point. If your partner raises your suit you may bid it as many times as you wish with only a four-card suit and many times you will play a hand at game with only four trumps in declarer's hand.

13-15 Point Rebids (Minimum Hand)

If you have the minimum opening count and your partner has bid another suit, you absolutely *must* bid again, but there are only three things you should do.

1) Bid one no trump. A bid of one no trump says, "Partner, that's it. I've nothing else to say."

Example:

♠ K 7 4
♡ J 8 2
◊ A Q 8 2
♣ K 6 4

You open the bidding with one diamond and your partner bids one heart. Your rebid should be one no trump to show a minimum count of 13-15 points and a balanced hand.

73

2) Raise partner's suit.

Example:

♠ K 8
♡ J 8 7 3
◇ A Q 10 7 6
♣ K 4

You open the bidding with one diamond and partner responds one heart. Your rebid should be two hearts. This says, "Partner, I'm minimum, but at least I like your suit. This is the best I can do."

3) Rebid your suit.

Example:

♠ K 5 3
♡ 7 2
◇ A K Q 9 5
♣ 10 9 5

You open the bidding with one diamond and your partner responds one heart. Your rebid should be two diamonds. This is another weak rebid to show minimum point count and at least a five-card suit. It tells your partner loud and clear that you have nothing else to offer.

When your partner has responded to your opening bid with one no trump or a raise in your suit, he has told you he is minimum — so, of course, you can pass.

Examples:

♠ K 8
♡ A J 10 6 5
◇ K J 2
♣ 5 3 2

You open the bidding with one heart and partner responds two hearts, which is a very weak response. Since

74

you have minimum point count and so does partner, you pass.

♠ Q J 2
♡ A J 6
◇ Q J 6 3
♣ K 10 8

You open the bidding with one diamond and partner responds with one no trump, showing even distribution and six to nine points. Since the hand will play in no trump and you are minimum and partner is also, pass.

16-20 Point Rebids (Good Hand)

If partner responds to your opening bid, a hand in this category should be investigating game. When you have 16-20 points, *don't make a minimum response.* You must be encouraging and let your partner know you're good by making a positive bid.

Examples:

♠ K Q
♡ Q 9 5 4
◇ A Q 10 4 3
♣ K 4

You open the bidding with one diamond and partner responds one heart. You have support for partner's major suit and 16-20 points. Jump to three hearts. If you bid two hearts, you are showing a minimum opening hand. Don't make a minimum rebid with 16-20 points. You are saying, "Partner, if you have a minimum six or seven points, we can't make a game, but if you have eight or nine (or more) won't you please bid game?"

♠ K 8 3
♡ K 6
◊ A Q J 6 5 2
♣ A 2

You open the bidding with one diamond and your partner bids one heart. Your rebid would be three diamonds. A two diamond rebid would show minimum opening count.

♠ K 6
♡ A J 7 5 2
◊ A Q 8 7
♣ Q 9

You open the bidding with one heart and your partner makes a weak response of two hearts. Your rebid is three hearts. You add your points to your partner's six to nine points. If your partner has the minimum, he should pass. If your partner has the maximum, you have 26 points and he should bid four hearts.

♠ K 9
♡ A J 6 5 4
◊ A Q 9 6
♣ A 3

You open the bidding with one heart and your partner responds two hearts. Your 20 points added to your partner's minimum six points should give you game in hearts. Jump to four hearts.

♠ A Q 8 7 3
♡ J 2
◊ A Q 7
♣ A 7 2

You open the bidding with one spade and your partner responds one no trump. Your rebid is two no trump. Your 17 points added to your partner's points will give you game in no trump only if he has the maximum count. He should pass if he is minimum and bid three no trump if he is maximum.

♠ A Q 8 5 4
♡ K 5
◊ A Q 2
♣ A 6 4

You open the bidding with one spade and your partner bids one no trump. In this case you are strong enough to jump to three no trump. Your 19 points added to your partner's count should give you a shot at game at three no trump.

♠ 7
♡ A K Q J 7 6
◊ A 10 8
♣ K Q 3

You open the bidding with one heart and your partner responds one no trump. That's all you need to know to jump to four hearts! Your partner has six to nine points. That should give you game at four hearts.

♠ A K 7
♡ A Q J 6
◊ Q J 7
♣ K 4 2

You open the bidding with one club (with 20 points, you are too strong to bid one no trump and too weak to bid

77

two no trump). Your partner responds with one no trump. Even if your partner has the minimum for a response, you should have game at three no trump.

Over 20 Point Rebids (Enormous Hand)

If you have an enormous hand with over 20 points, you would certainly be looking for game and possibly slam, depending on the response you get from your partner. The only way to show this high count is the jump shift. A jump shift simply means that you change suits and jump the bid one higher than necessary. *THE JUMP SHIFT IS FORCING TO GAME AND AN INVITATION TO SLAM.* It's rare that you have a hand this good, but we have to know what to do with it if we're lucky enough to get one! (For information on slam bidding, see the Blackwood convention in Chapter 6.)

Example:

♠ J 8
♡ A K Q 8 3
♢ 6
♣ A K Q 6 2

Open the bidding with one heart because when you have two biddable five-card suits, open with the higher ranking. Your partner says one spade. Your rebid is a jump shift to *three* clubs. This tells your partner you hold more than 20 points.

Test Yourself

In the following cases, you have opened the bidding

with one diamond and your partner has responded one spade. Before looking at the answers, try to determine your rebid.

1. ♠ Q 6 3 2
   ♡ K 4 3
   ◇ K J 6 4
   ♣ A 2

Two spades. You are telling your partner you have minimum opening count and 13-15 points.

2. ♠ Q 6 3 2
   ♡ K 10 4
   ◇ A K 6 4
   ♣ A 2

Three spades. You have a good hand and support for partner's suit. Don't bid two spades. It shows a minimum hand. Jump to three spades and correctly describe your hand to your partner.

3. ♠ A 2
   ♡ Q 10 4
   ◇ K Q 10 4
   ♣ Q 9 8 2

One no trump. This bid shows you are in the minimum range and have even distribution.

4. ♠ K 2
   ♡ K 10 2
   ◇ A K J 6 3
   ♣ 10 8 6

Two diamonds. Rebid your good five-card suit at the two level with minimum point count.

5. ♠ K 2
   ♡ Q 10 4
   ◇ A K J 6 3 2
   ♣ K 10

Three diamonds. With 16-20 points and at least a good five-card suit, jump to *three* diamonds. A rebid of two diamonds would show a minimum hand.

6. ♠ A
♡ A K Q J 8
◇ Q J 9 7 4 2
♣ 10

Three hearts. Your jump shift to three hearts shows over 20 points and forces your partner to keep bidding until you reach game. Slam might also be a possibility! Remember, you open with one diamond because when you have two biddable suits, bid the longer one first.

In the following cases, you have opened the bidding with one heart and partner bids two hearts.

7. ♠ 10 2
♡ A Q J 4 3
◇ K 10 4
♣ Q 10 6

Pass. You are minimum and so is your partner. This hand isn't going anywhere.

8. ♠ A 10
♡ K Q J 10 5
◇ K 9 3
♣ A 4 2

Three hearts. If partner has the minimum to respond, he will pass. If he has the maximum, he will bid four hearts (18 points plus partner's eight to nine points should produce a game at four hearts).

9. ♠ A 2
♡ A K Q J 2
◇ 10 8 3 2
♣ A 10

Four hearts. You know your partner has six points and support for your hearts. You add your 20 points to partner's six points and you have 26 points or a game at four hearts.

NOTES

NOTES

6
HIGH OPENING BIDS AND RESPONSES

Now, we're going to talk about two very different kinds of hands that should be opened with bids of two, three or four in a suit.

Without a doubt, the most exciting (and rare) hands in bridge are those beauties with enough points to make a game all by themselves with no help from partner. At first glance, you're so overwhelmed with your riches that you hardly know what to do. So, we're going to learn right now. We only wish these hands came along more often.

Another sort of hand that should be opened above the one level is a *very weak hand* with a long suit. The purpose of this preemptive bid is to make life difficult for your opponents.

We will also show partner's correct responses to these high opening bids.

Opening Two Bids
The opening bid of two of a suit is the strongest bid in

bridge and is a definite force bid to game. In other words, you and your partner must keep bidding until game has been reached. However, you must be sure you have adequate strength to open the bidding at the two level because your partner must keep bidding even if he doesn't have a point in his hand. There are two ways to determine if you have an opening two bid.

Count Your Points
Five-card suit and 25 points
Six-card suit and 23 points } Open the bidding
Seven-card suit and 21 points } with two of a suit

Count Your Losers
If you can count your losing cards and you are within one of making game in your hand, open the bidding with two of a suit. With long suits, you expect to catch your opponent's cards in that suit with your high ones, so eventually your small cards will win tricks. Again, remember that you are forcing your partner to bid and keep bidding until you reach game — even though he might not have one point in his hand.

Examples:

♠ A K Q J 10
♡ 3
◇ K Q J 5
♣ A K 4

This hand should open the bidding with two spades. If you count points, the hand has 25 points with a five-card suit. The hand also has only three probable losers — one heart, one diamond and one club. (Of course, you *may* lose two diamonds.)

85

♠ 4
♡ A
◇ A Q J 10 7
♣ A K J 6 5 2

Open the bidding with two clubs. The hand has 23 points and a six-card suit. Remember, if you have two biddable suits, open the longer suit. The hand will probably only lose one spade, one diamond and one club.

♠ 5
♡ A K J 6 4
◇ A K Q 6 3
♣ K 7

Open the bidding with two hearts. Remember, when you have two biddable five-card suits, open with the higher ranking. The hand only has three or perhaps four losers.

♠ A K Q J 7 6 4
♡ A 9 7
◇ A 8
♣ 5

Open the bidding with two spades. You have 21 points and a seven-card suit. There are only four probable losers— one club, one diamond, and two hearts.

Responses To Two Of A Suit

When your partner has opened the bidding with two of a suit, *YOU ARE FORCED TO KEEP BIDDING UNTIL THE PARTNERSHIP REACHES GAME.*

0-6 Points (Negative Response)

Bid two no trump. This bid tells your partner you have less than seven points. *Always* bid two no trump with less than seven points.

86

Over 6 Points (Positive Response)

With over six points, you can support partner's suit, bid a new suit, or bid *three* no trump (as opposed to the two no trump negative bid). We call these bids positive responses, and there is nothing that will make your partner happier than to learn that you have some high cards too.

Examples:

In the following three examples, your partner opens the bidding with two spades and holds:

♠ A K Q J 8 5
♡ A 3
◇ A K Q 3
♣ 2

♠ 8 5 4
♡ Q 8 6 4
◇ 10 8 6
♣ 7 3 2

Your response to your partner's two spade bid is two no trump. The bidding should go like this:
    Partner: Two spades.
    You: Two no trump.
    Partner: Three diamonds.
    You: Three spades.
    Partner: Four spades.
You must keep bidding until you get to game!

♠ 7 3
♡ Q 10 8 6 4 3 2
◇ 3
♣ 7 4 2

Your response to your partner's two spade bid is two no trump. The bidding should go like this:

Partner: Two spades.
You: Two no trump.
Partner: Three dia-monds.
You: Three hearts.
Partner: Three spades.
You: Four spades.

♠ 8 5 3
♡ K 10 8 4 3
◊ 7 6 2
♣ A 6

You hold eight points and your *positive* response to partner's two spade bid is three hearts. The bidding should go like this:

Partner: Two spades.
You: Three Hearts.
Partner: Four diamonds.
You: Four spades.

Your partner might then investigate a slam through the Blackwood convention discussed next.

Blackwood Convention

The Blackwood convention allows you and your partner to investigate whether or not you have a slam. The convention bid for Blackwood is *FOUR NO TRUMP*. Four no trump is an artificial bid which has nothing to do with no trump. It asks, "Partner. how many aces do you have?"

Responses To Four No Trump Bid (Blackwood Convention)

When your partner bids four no trump to ask about your aces, you answer in the following manner. It couldn't be simpler!

No aces — bid five clubs
One ace — bid five diamonds
Two aces — bid five hearts
Three Aces — bid five spades
Four aces — bid five clubs

Notice that the five club bid indicates either all of the aces or none of them. There is no chance in the world of getting mixed up between the two. Usually the person who asks for aces has at least one, so there is no problem. If the Blackwood bidder has no aces and his partner bids five clubs, he can be sure it means all four aces or the partnership would never have bid so much.

It is important to remember the bonuses for bidding and making a slam to see the advantages of investigating a slam whenever it seems possible.

SLAM BONUSES

	Not Vulnerable	Vulnerable
Small slam (all but 1 trick)	500 points	750 points
Grand slam (all tricks)	1,000 points	1,500 points

Examples:

♠ A K Q 8 5 4
♡ A K J 4
◇ A 3
♣ 7

Your opening bid is two spades. You have only three probable losers in the hand. Let's say your partner responds positively with three diamonds indicating at least seven points. Your bid is then three hearts and your partner then supports your first suit with three spades. Slam is a definite possibility. You have agreed on a suit and if your partner has two of your three losers covered, you have a slam at six or seven spades. Your next bid is *four no trump* to find out how many aces he has. Your partner bids five clubs showing no aces. You then bid six spades (small slam) because you are missing one of the aces but partner will have other support because he has at least seven points.

Preemptive Bids

A preemptive bid is the *very weakest opening bid* you can make. It is used when your hand is too weak to open the bidding with one. Now you will ask yourself, "Why in the world should I open the bidding at three or four if I'm not strong enough to even bid one?" The answer is very simple. When your hand is so weak, the chances are great that the opponents have a lot of strength and you should be eager to make it very hard for them to bid. There are two rules you should keep in mind for these bids — you never preempt unless you have at least a seven-card suit and you always bid as high as you possibly can because you *never* bid again.

The important thing to remember with a preemptive bid is that it is a defensive bid. *YOU DON'T EXPECT*

TO MAKE IT — YOU ARE SACRIFICING TO KEEP YOUR OPPONENTS FROM MAKING A GAME.

But, how do you know how high to open? There is a simple rule — count your losing cards and if you are not vulnerable, bid three more than you think you can make. If you are vulnerable, bid two more than you think you can make. This is because you fully expect your opponents to double the bid, and you are perfectly willing to lose 500 points but no more.

Remember, if you are vulnerable that means you have one game toward winning the rubber. Not vulnerable means that you have no game toward winning the rubber. This distinction is important because there are large penalties if you are vulnerable and you don't make your bid. If you are not vulnerable and the opponents double your bid and set you three tricks, they get 500 points — 100 for the first trick you go down, and 200 for each additional trick you are set. However, if you are vulnerable, the penalty for not making your contract is 200 for the first trick you are set and 300 points for each additional trick. So, you can only afford to go down two tricks when vulnerable.

Examples:

♠ A Q J 7 5 4 3
♡ 6
♢ 10 8 3
♣ 7 4

You are not vulnerable. Open the bidding with three spades. You will probably lose one spade trick and all hearts, diamonds, and clubs. You think you can take six tricks so your bid is three more than you think you can make or three spades. If your opponents want to enter the bid-

ding, they will have to do so
at the four level.

♠ 4
♡ 10 8
◇ K Q J 9 7 6 5 3
♣ 6 2

You are not vulnerable. You
should make seven diamond
tricks and lose the rest. Therefore, open the bidding with
four diamonds (three more
tricks than you think you can
make).

Responses To Preemptive Bids

When your partner opens with a preemptive bid, the
first thing you do is look at the score pad to see whether
or not you are vulnerable so you will know whether
your partner plans to be set two tricks or three tricks. If
you have enough tricks for game when added to your
partner's hand — bid it. Otherwise, pass. When your
partner opens with a preemptive bid, you should *never*
change the suit. Either raise him or pass because he has
already told you by his bid that his hand is worthless
unless played in his suit.

Of course, if the opponents bid over your partner's
preempt, you *will* raise your partner if you have a trick
(an ace or a king-queen) in your hand. If you have two
tricks, and it's necessary, you may raise him twice
because you'll still just get set the same number of tricks
he was planning to lose in the first place.

Examples:

In the following examples, assume your partner has
preempted with three spades and you are not
vulnerable. Your opponents have passed.

92

♠ 9 3
♡ 8 3 2
◇ A K Q 8 6 2
♣ K 2

You should pass. Don't bid the diamond suit! When your partner has preempted, don't change suits. Your three tricks in diamonds should enable your partner to make his bid.

♠ 7
♡ A 9 3
◇ A K 7 6 5
♣ K Q 6 3

Bid four spades. You have four probable tricks. It is not necessary for you to have support in spades because your partner has at least seven in his suit. Three of your tricks will take care of the three your partner was planning to be set, and your fourth trick enables you to raise him.

♠ 2
♡ A K Q 7 5 4 3
◇ 7 4 2
♣ 5 2

You should pass. If you had been the first bidder, you would have opened with three hearts. But you shouldn't change the suit after your partner has preempted with three spades and you only have three probable tricks.

Test Yourself

You are the dealer and you are vulnerable. Before looking at the answers, try to determine what your opening bid will be.

1. ♠ A K Q J 5 3 2
   ♡ A 7 2
   ◇ K Q
   ♣ A

   Two spades. You have only three probable losers — two hearts and one diamond.

2. ♠ A K 10 4
   ♡ Q 3 2
   ◇ A
   ♣ A Q 10 4 3

   One club. It is a beautiful hand but you simply don't have enough points to open at the two level.

3. ♠ A K Q 8 4
   ♡ A Q J 4 3
   ◇ A
   ♣ K 3

   Two spades. With 26 points you can open at the two level. Since you have two biddable five-card suits, the rule is to bid the higher ranking suit first.

4. ♠ A Q J 6 5 4 3 2
   ♡ 3 2
   ◇ 10 4
   ♣ 6

   Three spades. You will probably make all but one of your spade tricks and lose the rest. You are vulnerable so bid two tricks more than you think you can make and preempt with three spades. If you hadn't been vulnerable, you would have opened with four spades.

5. ♠ 10 8
   ♡ A Q J 10 7 6 4
   ◇ A Q 6
   ♣ 4

   One heart. You have too many points to preempt. With opening count and a seven-card suit, open the bidding at the one level.

6. ♠ 7 6
   ♡ 10 8
   ◇ K 4
   ♣ A Q 10 7 6 4 3

   Three clubs. You should be able to make seven tricks. Since you are vulnerable, bid two tricks more than you can make and bid three clubs.

7. ♠ A K J 10 8 3
   ♡ A K J 10 4
   ◇ A
   ♣ 2

   Two spades. When you have two biddable suits, bid the longer suit first. With 24 points and a six-card suit, you have enough to open the bidding at the two level.

Your partner has opened the bidding with two spades and your opponent has passed. What is your bid?

8. ♠ 6 2
   ♡ K 10 9 8 4 3
   ◇ 10 6
   ♣ 8 7 4

   Two no trump. Two no trump is a bid which tells your partner you have less than seven points. It has nothing to do with no trump — it only shows point count.

9. ♠ Q 10 4 3
   ♡ K 4
   ◇ Q 6 3 2
   ♣ 10 8 3

   Three spades. This is a positive response showing over six points and support for partner's suit.

10. ♠ J 10 8
    ♡ Q 7 3
    ◇ 10 8 6 4
    ♣ K 8 6

    Two no trump. With less than seven points, bid two no trump.

11. ♠ K 10
    ♡ Q J 8 6
    ◇ K 4 2
    ♣ 6 5 4 3

Three no trump. Two no trump would indicate less than seven points. With balanced distribution and more than six points, bid three no trump.

12. ♠ K 2
    ♡ A J 10 8 7 6
    ◇ 10 5 3
    ♣ 3 2

Three hearts. Respond positively with your six-card suit.

Your partner has opened the bidding with three spades and you are not vulnerable. Your opponent has passed. What is your bid?

13. ♠ 3 2
    ♡ A K Q 4
    ◇ 10 9 8 7
    ♣ 8 6 5

Pass. Your three heart tricks should enable your partner to make his bid exactly. Since the partnership is not vulnerable, your partner has bid three more tricks than he thinks he can make.

14. ♠ A 3 2
    ♡ A J 10 8
    ◇ 6 4
    ♣ A K 4 2

Four spades. Your four tricks should enable your partner to make game. You can take care of his deficit of three, plus one more trick for the raise.

15. ♠ 4
   ♡ A K 10 8 4 3 2
   ◇ A 4
   ♣ 10 8 4

Pass. Don't bid your seven-card heart suit. Remember, when your partner has preempted, don't change suits. Your three probable tricks should enable your partner to make his bid.

NOTES

NOTES

99

7

OPENING LEADS
AND PLAY OF THE HAND

THE OPENING LEAD is the most important play in any hand. It is so vital that the experts have estimated that half of the contracts that are made at the bridge table could have been defeated by the opponents if they had made the perfect opening lead. And half the contracts that are defeated could have been made if the opening lead had been a poor one.

Sometimes you are delighted to be the opening leader. You know exactly what you wish to lead, and can hardly wait! Other times it is a real burden. Your hand just doesn't contain a good opening lead and you're in a quandary. So, often it comes down to the process of elimination and a choice of the lesser of evils.

There are charts you can memorize that will help you with a decision on what in the world to lead, but I think memorizing is a terrific bore. It's a lot easier just to learn the principles behind leads and have an idea of what you're trying to accomplish and what's the best way to go about it. Of course the object is to try your best to defeat the opponents' contract. If the opponents are playing the hand at no trump, your lead will be very different from the lead you might make if they were playing the hand in a suit contract. If there has been a lot of bidding during the auction, it is tremendously helpful to you. But first let's consider a lead when you have gained absolutely no information from the bidding.

Leading Against A No Trump Contract

Your opponent has opened the bidding with one no trump, his partner raises to two no trump, and he bids three no trump. Usually in no trump, it's a race between the two teams to see who can set up a long suit and take tricks eventually with small cards. If you have a five-card suit with an honor, it's a pretty good idea to lead it and hope for future tricks. Now we get to *which* card you will lead in the suit. Suppose you hold K 10 7 6 5. Obviously, the 5, 6, and 7 are all the same value, so it wouldn't appear to make any difference which one you lead, but believe me it does! Remember, this is a partnership game, as we've stressed constantly, and you're always eager to give your partner information.

The Rule of 11 is a very helpful little thing to know about — and it *always* works! Here it is — if you lead the fourth best card in your long suit, your partner can subtract the spots on the card (in this case the six) from 11 and the answer tells him how many cards higher than the six there are in the three hands other than the leader's. Your partner can see the dummy hand and his own hand, so he knows exactly how many cards declarer has in that suit that are higher than the six. You will lead the fourth best card in your longest suit often against a no trump bid, so let's remember it.

101

Now we'll consider some hands that don't have a five-card suit. Very often you're not that lucky!

Examples:

The opponents have bid three no trump and you hold this hand:

♠ K J 7 5
♡ J 10 9 5
♢ 7 3
♣ 7 4 3

Pretty bad, isn't it? But not hopeless. The first thing you know is that you do NOT want to lead a spade. With just four cards in the suit and a tenace, you want someone else to lead the suit so perhaps you'll take tricks with both the king and the jack. A tenace is two high cards with the one in the middle missing. There is no reason to lead a diamond or club, but a very good reason to lead a heart! You have a sequence in that suit. A sequence is holding three cards adjacent in rank, and you always lead the top of the rank, so in this case you lead the jack of hearts.

♠ K 10 5
♡ J 6 5 2
♢ A Q 10 3
♣ 10 9

This is a lesser of evils hand. We certainly would *NEVER* lead a diamond from the A Q 10 tenace. We'd rather have someone else lead a spade so we'd have a better

102

chance of taking a trick with the king. If we lead the fourth best heart, partner might think we had something better and would like him to lead it back to us. Not true! So, we lead the 10 of clubs because at least partner will know when we lead the 10, we have nothing higher and are not interested in clubs.

♠ 10 7 4
♡ 10 8 6 3 2
◊ 7 6
♣ 7 4 2

A miserable little hand, but we all get these sometimes, and the best lead is the 10 of spades. No sense fooling with the hopeless hearts, and if you lead a heart your partner might think you want him to lead it back. The only hope for taking tricks is in your partner's hand, and he might have some good spades, because if the opponents had them all, they'd probably have bid them.

If your partner has bid during the auction and the opponents are playing the hand in no trump, it's wise to lead your partner's suit. Now you only need to decide which card to lead. If you have only two cards in his suit, lead the high one. If you have three small cards lead the highest.

Examples:
Ax, Kx, xx, xxx.

If you hold three cards to an honor be sure you lead low, and you always lead the lowest card if you have four in your partner's suit. There is only one exception. If you have four cards with two touching honors, lead high.

Examples:
Axx, Kxx, Qxx, Axxx
QJxx, J10xx

If you and your partner have both bid during the auction, I would probably lead my partner's suit instead of my own. It will make him happy, and besides, if we don't manage to set the opponents, he could never think to himself, "I'll bet if my partner had led my suit they wouldn't have made their bid." Of course he'd never *say* this, because we're always gentle and kind to our partners, aren't we?

If your partner has bid a suit, and then he doubles the opponents' no trump contract, you have *no choice* but to lead his suit. He is saying, "Partner, if you'll lead my suit, we'll set them." So of course you do, even though you have a singleton.

Example:

♠ 8
♡ K Q J 9 4
◇ 9 4 2
♣ 7 6 5 2

Partner has doubled the no trump bid after having bid spades. If he had not doubled, I would have happily led my king of hearts, but when he doubles, I lead the singleton in his suit.

If your partner doubles a no trump contract when he has not bid but you have, he is saying, "Partner, please lead your suit."

Example:

♠ K J 7 5 2
♡ K Q J 7
◇ A 8
♣ 7 4

If partner had not doubled, I would have opened the king of hearts, but because he doubled, I lead the five of spades — the fourth best of the suit I bid.

Leading Against A Suit Contract

When the opponents are playing the hand at a suit contract, your thinking is very different from defending against a no trump contract. You know that you won't take any tricks with small cards because the opponent will be able to trump them. For instance, if you had K Q 6 4 2 in a suit and the bid was no trump, your lead would be the four, hoping to get lots of tricks later. But with the same cards and the opponent playing the hand at a suit bid, you would lead the king to get rid of the ace, hoping your queen would take the second trick in that suit.

When your partner has bid a suit and you have only two cards in that suit, lead high — just as you did against the no trump. If you have three cards with an honor, lead low as against the no trump contract *except* if you have the ace of your partner's suit, you lead it, because the opponent will probably be able to trump the suit soon, and you don't want to take a chance that he will trump your ace.

The top of a sequence is always a good, safe lead.

Holding king, queen, jack, you lead the king. Holding queen, jack, 10, you lead the queen.

Many people think a singleton is a choice lead against a suit bid. Sometimes it is the best possible lead, and sometimes it is very poor.

Examples:

♠ A 5 3
♡ K 9 7 5
◊ 4
♣ 9 7 4 3 2

My partner has bid hearts and the opponents are playing the hand in spades. I lead the singleton diamond because I know I can get in the lead early with the ace of trumps. Then I will lead my partner's suit hoping he has the ace, and he will lead a diamond back to me which I can trump.

♠ A 10 7 5
♡ 9
◊ Q J 10 8 5
♣ 8 4 2

The contract is spades, and this hand should NEVER lead his singleton heart. Having as many as four of the opponents' trumps, you should lead your long suit hoping to make *him* trump. You can do him more damage by having as many trumps as he has than you can by trumping a trick. Remember that this is a very potent weapon to wield.

When you have a natural trump trick, such as Kx or Qxx, it is unwise to lead your singleton. By natural trump trick we mean that we expect to take a trick with the king or queen because they are guarded by small cards that will fall on the honors. If you have a spare trump that you don't need, such as Kxx, it's a good lead, and certainly with two or three useless little trumps it is acceptable. You will always lead your singleton if it is the suit your partner has bid.

The lead of a doubleton is not one of my favorites by any means and it is usually led when anything else would be even more unattractive.

Example:

♠ 8 6	You don't want to lead hearts,
♡ A 10 4 3	diamonds, or clubs, so just
◊ A 10 8 6	lead the doubleton because
♣ A Q 7	it's the lesser of evils.

I'm sure you've heard the old expression, "When in doubt lead trumps." Well, just forget it! Sometimes the lead of the trump suit is the very best lead you can possibly make — but never when in doubt. The bidding will indicate whether the trump lead will be brilliant. If both of the opponents have bid suits, and they finally get together on a third suit, it sounds like they may have short suits and want to trump some losing tricks, so by leading the trumps you could well be upsetting their plans.

I very much dislike leading an ace. If you do, what do you catch? A bunch of *little* cards, and it's much more profitable to wait for someone else to lead that suit and catch a big card with your ace. It is also bad to lead *from* an ace at a suit contract, so just lead another suit instead.

There's an old saying, "Never lead from a king." Don't let that worry you. Of course it isn't your favorite lead, but, as we have seen, sometimes you have *very* hard choices and if I had to lead from one of these suits — Kxx or Qxx — I'd much prefer to lead from the king than the queen. The king has a greater chance to survive.

Whenever you lead a king, your partner knows you have either the ace or the queen. There would be no other reason to lead it. With AKxx you always lead the king first. If you ever lead the ace followed by the king your partner knows it's a doubleton and you can trump the next time.

As you can see, this business of the opening lead can be a real problem, but we all just do the best we can.

Bridge Play

Playing a hand of bridge is fascinating whether you are a declarer or defender. Each hand you play is different from any you've ever seen before, so there's no way in the world the game could get dull. There is so much you will learn about playing as time goes on, but there are a few tips that will make the learning process easier and more fun.

If you are declarer, there is one moment that you should take time to very carefully plan your strategy, and that is when the opening lead is made and your partner's hand goes down on the board. Look the two hands over, and if you are playing at no trump *count your winners*. If you have bid game (three no trump), that means you must take nine tricks. Very rarely will you be able to count nine winners, so you must decide right then what will be the best way to try to develop tricks so you can make your contract. If you are playing the hand at a game in a major suit, *count your losers* (the cards that you can't avoid losing). You know you're just supposed to lose three tricks if you make your contract, so plan right now the best way to avoid losing tricks. Sometimes it is best to lead your trump suit and get the opponents' trumps — especially if you have another good suit in one of the hands so you'll be able to throw away some of your losers on those good cards. But sometimes you might need your trumps so you can trump losers in one hand, and it's best not to lead the trumps immediately. This is a matter of judgment, and the more you play the better your judgment will become. Remember, we *all* make mistakes, so don't worry about it. Nobody's perfect, but please, just go on and play! Nothing is more boring than a slow player! After you plan your strategy, just get the show on the road, and play fast. You know, usually this business of hesitating over every play is just a habit — and a bad one — so let's avoid it!

When you're declarer and you have a good suit with high cards in both hands, it's good to get into the practice of playing the high cards from the short hand first, so you will end up in the hand with more cards.

Sometimes you have a tenace suit (cards headed by the ace, queen). One of the opponents has the king and you don't know which one, but it is important that you lead a low card *up to* a queen so that hand will be the third hand to play, and if the king is on the left side, you'll get tricks with both the ace and the queen. This is called a "finesse," and you just *hope* the missing high card will be where you want it. We play the combination of KJxx the same way and hope the queen will be in the right place.

As you play the hand, try to watch and notice what cards your opponents discard when they cannot follow suit. This will help you figure out where some of the high cards are.

When you are defending, the play of the hand is just as exciting, even though declarer surely has better cards than you have. There are lots of ways you can give information about your hand to your partner. For instance, when he makes the opening lead, if you like the suit and want him to continue with it, you try to play a rather high card, like the six, seven or eight, on his lead, and that says, "Come on partner — I like it!" If you play a two, three, or four, he will know that you're not very enthusiastic about that suit. If he should lead a low card in a suit and you happen to have touching honors (KQx or QJx or J10x) be *sure* to play the lower of the touching honors. When we lead touching honors we always lead the high one, but when we play to someone else's lead we always play the low one.

When you cannot follow suit and must throw away a card in another suit, your partner will be watching to see what your discard will be — so discard a smaller card if you don't wish to have that suit led, and if you discard a larger card, your partner will know you have some strength in that suit.

There is an old saying, "Second hand plays low," and this is usually true unless there is a good reason not to. Also, "Third hand plays high" is usually true, though this too is a judgment thing, and you will soon learn when it is wise to ignore the old adages. Another old saying, "Cover an honor with an honor," is sometimes good advice — sometimes not. For instance, if the QJ10 of a suit is in the dummy hand and declarer leads the queen, of course you would not put your king on it. That would make it much too easy for the opponent to take it with the ace.

As the play of the hand goes on, suppose you take a trick and must lead. You have no clue from your partner about what he'd like, but it's your turn to lead and it can't be avoided, so you might let the dummy hand decide for you. If dummy is on your left, choose his strongest suit, and bravely lead it. If on right, lead dummy's weakest suit. This little old-fashioned verse is just as true as when it was written —

If Dummy's sitting on your right,
Lead the weakest thing in sight.
If Dummy on your left should be,
Through strength to partner. Do you see?

There are so *many* fine points in playing the hand and we have barely scratched the surface — just as we couldn't possibly cover all the bidding situations. That's one of the great things about this game — you keep on learning all the time. I do hope our time together has given you a good start and that you will enjoy playing more and more. You know, it's wonderful therapy! You're so busy thinking about what to bid, what to lead, how to play, that it's impossible to give a thought to problems that may be bothering you in the real world. Isn't it great to have something to do that's fun and also completely absorbing! Never forget that bridge is for pleasure, so don't dream of being upset by mistakes that you make — and I'm sure you'll never let anyone else's mistakes bother you. Remember, it's a lot more important to be known as the most pleasant player in town than as the best! And, who knows, someday you may be both!

Test Yourself

Before looking at the answers, try to determine your lead.

1. The opponents have bid four hearts.

♠ A 9 8 6 4
♡ J 10 7 3
◊ 2
♣ K 5 3

I would not lead the singleton diamond because I have four good trumps. I would not lead from the king of clubs because I would prefer that lead come to me. So, much as I dislike leading aces, I would lead the ace of spades because I have five and I hope declarer may be short and have to trump a spade soon, which would whittle his trump suit down to my size.

2. During the auction, my partner has bid diamonds, and then has doubled the opponents' three no trump.

♠ Q J 10 9 6 5
♡ 8 5 3
◊ 4
♣ 9 6 5

I must lead my singleton diamond because partner has doubled and told me to lead his suit. So, even though I don't like it, I shall certainly cooperate with partner.

3. The opponents have bid three no trump.

♠ K 8 7 5 4
♡ A K 2
♢ 9 5 4
♣ 10 4

I would lead the five of spades, and be very thankful that I have a five-card suit. By subtracting five from 11, my partner can tell how many spades higher than the five are in declarer's hand, because I led my fourth best card in the suit.

4. The opponents have bid four spades.

♠ 4
♡ K 7 3 2
♢ Q 6 4 3
♣ Q J 10 9

I have no problems about a lead in this hand because I have a sequence in the club suit, so of course I lead the queen of clubs — top of the sequence.

5. The opponents have bid spades.

♠ K Q 5
♡ 9 4
♢ A Q 8 2
♣ Q 9 7 3

I certainly won't lead spades, and I'll never lead diamonds from a tenace. I don't want to lead a small club so I shall lead the nine of hearts — *not* because it is a doubleton, but because I don't wish to lead anything else.

113

6. Spades are trump — this hand is almost like the last one.

♠ K Q 6
♡ 9 8 4
◇ A Q 3 2
♣ Q 9 5

The best lead in this hand is the nine of hearts. It is the "top of nothing" and partner will know I have no high cards in the suit. I lead this because everything else is worse.

7. The opponents have bid four hearts.

♠ 9 6 4
♡ 7 4 3
◇ 8
♣ K 9 6 4 3 2

This hand is so hopeless that I'm glad to have the singleton diamond to lead, because it doesn't look like there's a chance of taking a trick anywhere else.

8. The opponents have bid three no trump.

♠ 7 3 2
♡ A Q 10 6 2
◇ 9 8 4
♣ 6 3

I have a five-card suit with a tenace. If there were only four hearts in the hand I would lead the nine of diamonds, but with five hearts I am willing to lead from the tenace suit to hope for future tricks. I lead the six of hearts.

114

9. My partner has bid diamonds and the opponents have the contract at three no trump.

♠ J 10 9 4
♡ 8 3
◇ K 6 2
♣ Q 5 4 3

My lead is the two of diamonds. I have three of my partner's suit with an honor, so I lead low.

10. The opponents have bid four spades.

♠ 8 6 4
♡ K Q 9 2
◇ 5 3
♣ J 9 8 4

There is no problem in this hand, and I'm glad to have touching honors so I can lead the king, planning to lose it to the ace, but my queen will take the second trick in the heart suit.

NOTES

NOTES

117

GLOSSARY OF BRIDGE TERMS

Above the line — scoring points that don't count toward game.

Below the line — scoring points that count toward game.

Blackwood — a convention used to investigate slam possibilities.

Book — the first six tricks taken by declarer.

Convention — an unnatural bid.

Cue bid — an artificial bid demanding game.

Deal — distribution of 13 cards to each player in a clockwise manner.

Declarer — player who wins the contract and plays the hand.

Defender — opponent of the declarer.

Discard — playing a card of another suit when you cannot follow suit on the lead.

Distribution — the way cards are divided into suits.

Doubleton — two cards in a suit.

Down — failing to make the bid contracted.

118

Dummy — declarer's partner.

Finesse — trying to win a trick when there is a higher card in one of the opponent's hands.

Follow suit — playing a card of the same suit as the lead card.

Fourth hand — the player on the dealer's right.

Game — contract or contracts which score 100 points.

Grand slam — contract to take all 13 tricks.

Honor cards — any ace, king, queen, jack, or ten.

Jump — bidding more than necessary.

Jump shift — jump bid in a new suit.

Lead — the first card played to a trick.

Major suits — spades or hearts.

Make — take the number of tricks bid.

Minor suits — diamonds or clubs.

No trump — a contract when there is no trump suit.

Not vulnerable — partnership which has not scored a game.

Opening bid — first bid of a hand.

Opening lead — first lead of a hand.

Overcall — a bid over opponent's bid.

Overtricks — tricks made by declarer over the contract.

Part score — score less than game below the line.

Preemptive bid — a high-level bid on a weak hand.

Raise — a bid in the same suit as partner has bid.

Rebid — player's second chance to bid.

Responder — partner of the opening bidder.

Rubber — when one partnership wins two games.

Rule of 11 — the lead of the fourth best of a long suit against a no trump contract to aid partner in placing the cards.

Second hand — player on dealer's left.

Sequence — three cards in rank order (queen, jack, ten or ten, nine, eight, for example).

Small slam — a contract to take all but one trick.

Singleton — one card in a suit.

Stayman club convention — a convention used by partner of opening no trump bidder.

Take-out double — double made to force partner to bid.

Tenace — two honors not in sequence (ace, queen, for example).

Third hand — dealer's partner.

Trick — four cards played - one from each hand.

Trump — suit named in the final contract.

Void — having no cards in a suit.

Vulnerable — partnership which has scored one game toward the rubber.